MAX AXIOM
AND THE SOCIETY OF SUPER SCIENTISTS

EXPLORING VIRTUAL REALITY

BY *THOMAS K. ADAMSON*

ILLUSTRATED BY *DANIEL PEDROSA*

CAPSTONE PRESS
a capstone imprint

Published by Capstone Press, an imprint of Capstone.
1710 Roe Crest Drive
North Mankato, Minnesota 56003
capstonepub.com

Library of Congress Cataloging-in-Publication Data
Names: Adamson, Thomas K., 1970- author. | Pedrosa, Daniel, illustrator.
Title: Exploring virtual reality / by Thomas K. Adamson ; illustrated by Daniel Pedrosa.
Description: North Mankato, Minnesota : Capstone Press, an imprint of Capstone, [2024] | Series: Max Axiom and the society of super scientists Includes bibliographical references. | Audience: Ages 8 to 11 | Audience: Grades 4-6
Summary: "Have you ever wanted to travel to other planets? Maybe you'd like to dive to the bottom of the sea or walk among the dinosaurs. These things don't seem possible. But with virtual reality they can seem real. Strap on a pair of goggles and grab a controller to fight in space battles, fly over mountains, or even take a trip inside the human body. In this nonfiction graphic novel, Max Axiom and the Society of Super Scientists take a tour through the wonders of virtual reality to learn how it works, how it's used today, and what it might look like in the future"-- Provided by publisher.
Identifiers: LCCN 2022051418 (print) | LCCN 2022051419 (ebook) ISBN 9781669017219 (hardcover) | ISBN 9781669017165 (paperback) ISBN 9781669017172 (ebook pdf) | ISBN 9781669017196 (kindle edition) ISBN 9781669017202 (epub)
Subjects: LCSH: Virtual reality--Juvenile literature.
Classification: LCC QA76.9.A94 A36 2024 (print) | LCC QA76.9.A94 (ebook) DDC 006.8--dc23/eng/20230104
LC record available at https://lccn.loc.gov/2022051418
LC ebook record available at https://lccn.loc.gov/2022051419

Editorial Credits
Editor: Aaron Sautter; Designer: Elyse White;
Media Researcher: Rebekah Hubstenberger;
Production Specialist: Whitney Schaefer

All internet sites appearing in back matter were available and accurate when this book was sent to press.

TABLE OF CONTENTS

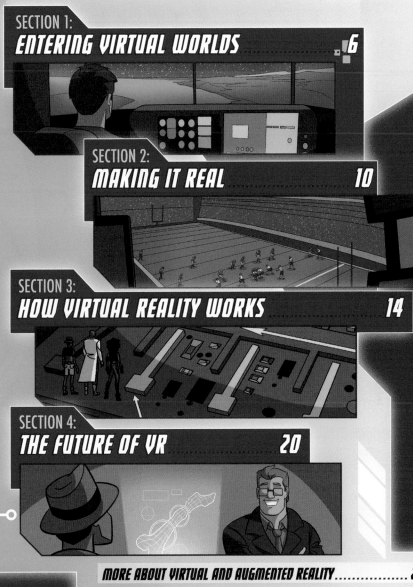

THE SOCIETY OF SUPER SCIENTISTS

MAX AXIOM

After years of study, Max Axiom, the world's first Super Scientist, knew the mysteries of the universe were too vast for one person alone to uncover. So Max created the Society of Super Scientists! Using their superpowers and super-smarts, this talented group investigates today's most urgent scientific and environmental issues and learns about actions everyone can take to solve them.

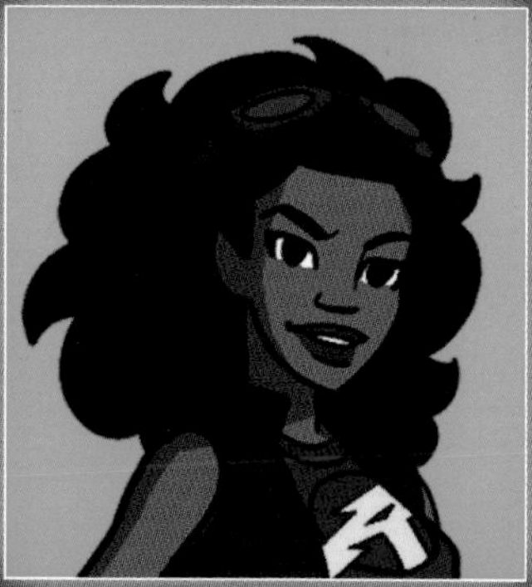

LIZZY AXIOM

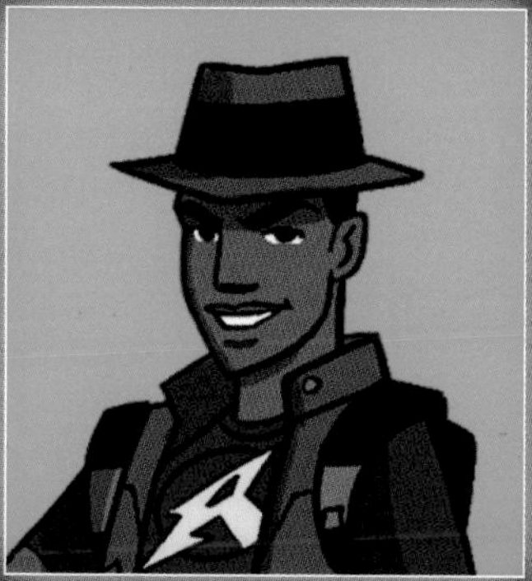

NICK AXIOM

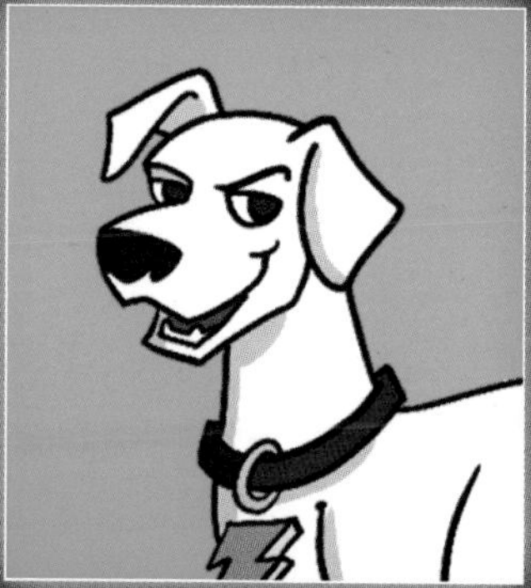

SPARK

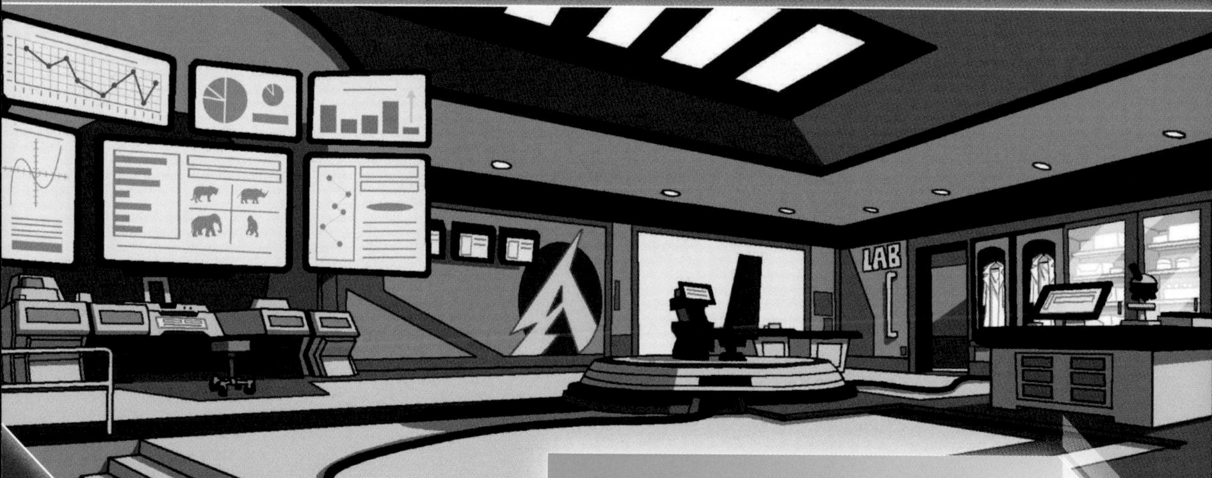

LAB

THE DISCOVERY LAB

Home of the Society of Super Scientists, this state-of-the-art lab houses advanced tools for cutting-edge research and radical scientific innovation. More importantly, it is a space for Super Scientists to collaborate and share knowledge as they work together to tackle any challenge.

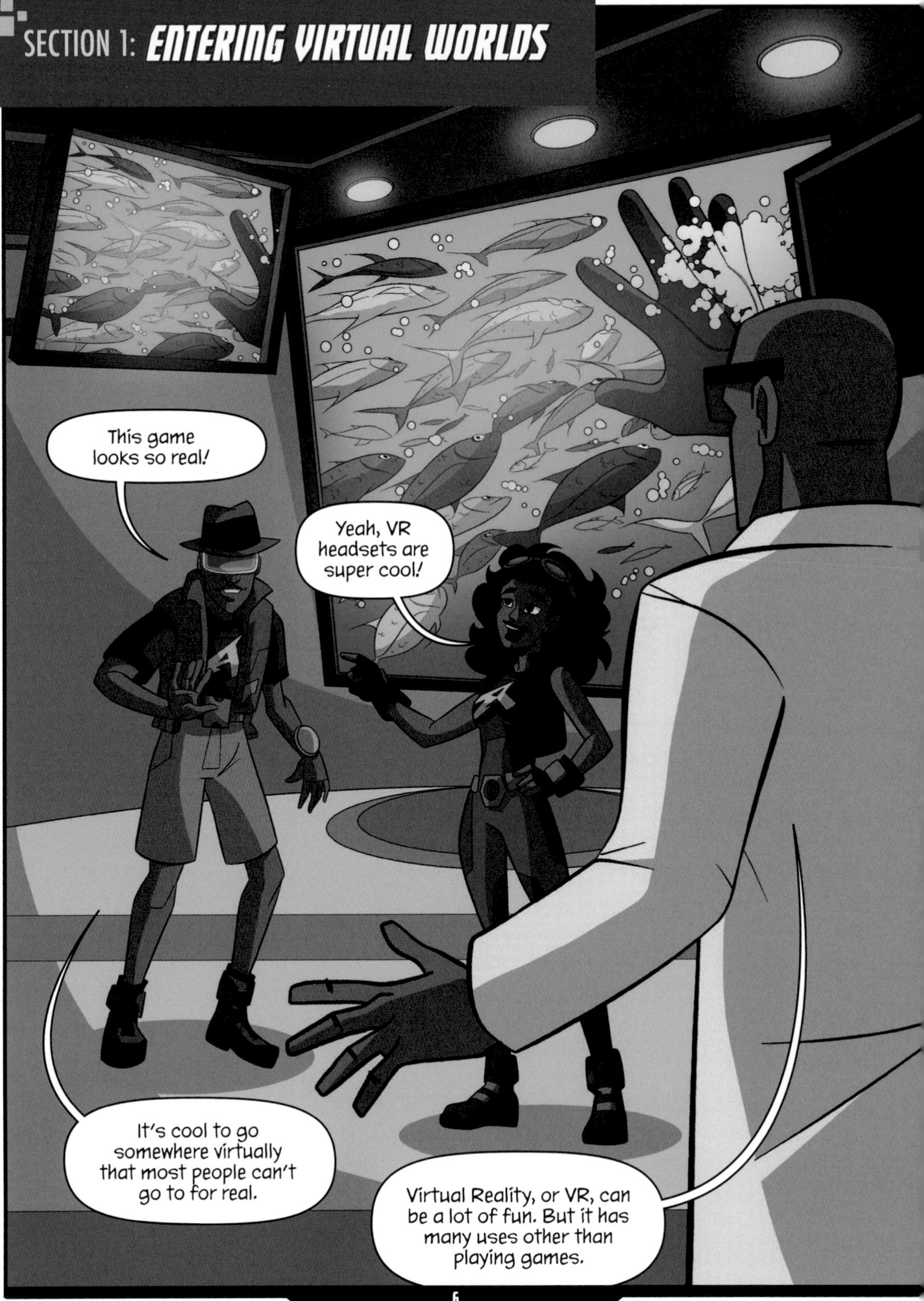
This game looks so real!
Yeah, VR headsets are super cool!
It's cool to go somewhere virtually that most people can't go to for real.
Virtual Reality, or VR, can be a lot of fun. But it has many uses other than playing games.

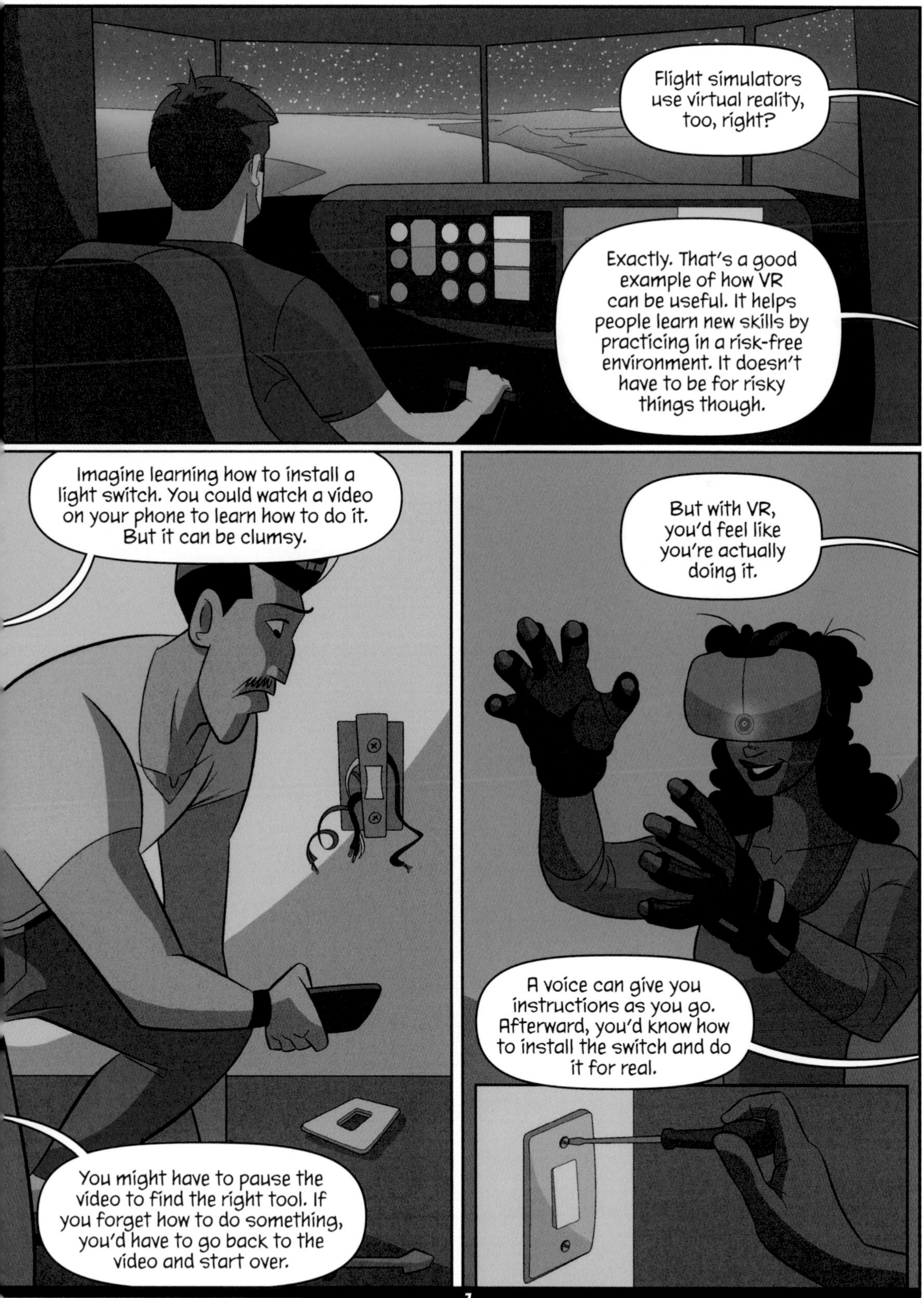
Flight simulators use virtual reality, too, right?
Exactly. That's a good example of how VR can be useful. It helps people learn new skills by practicing in a risk-free environment. It doesn't have to be for risky things though.
Imagine learning how to install a light switch. You could watch a video on your phone to learn how to do it. But it can be clumsy.
You might have to pause the video to find the right tool. If you forget how to do something, you'd have to go back to the video and start over.
But with VR, you'd feel like you're actually doing it.
A voice can give you instructions as you go. Afterward, you'd know how to install the switch and do it for real.

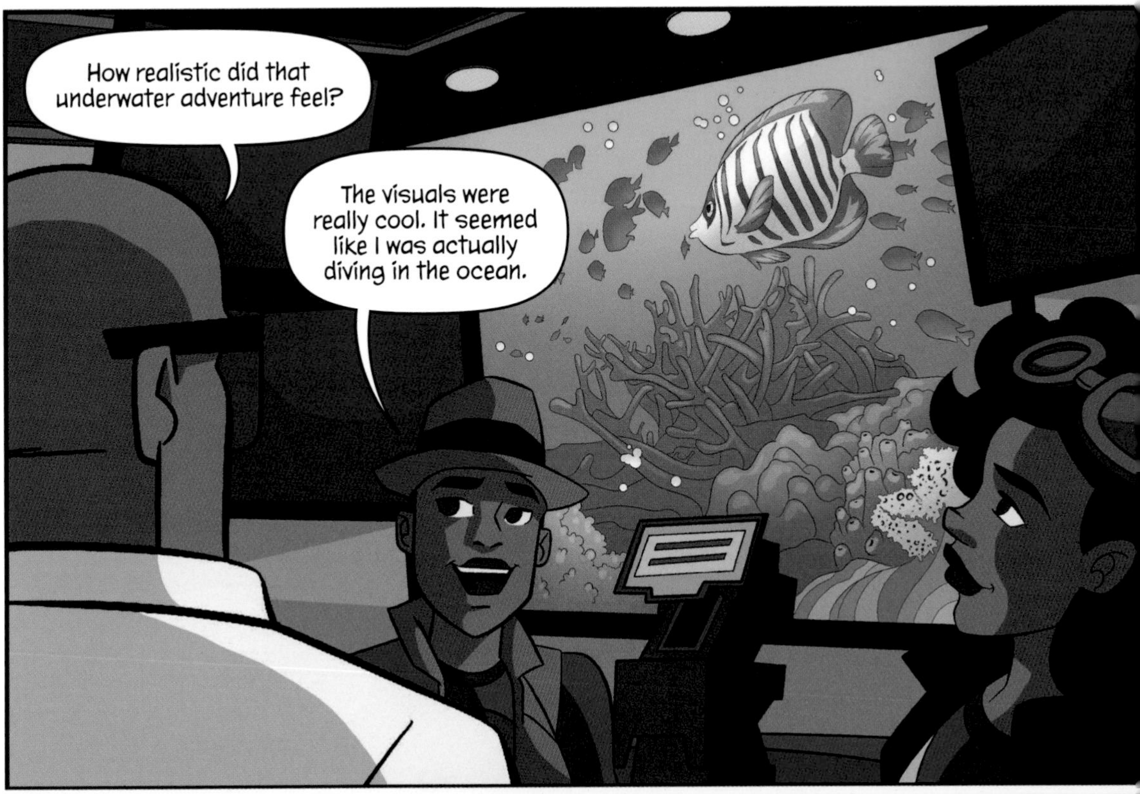
How realistic did that underwater adventure feel?
The visuals were really cool. It seemed like I was actually diving in the ocean.

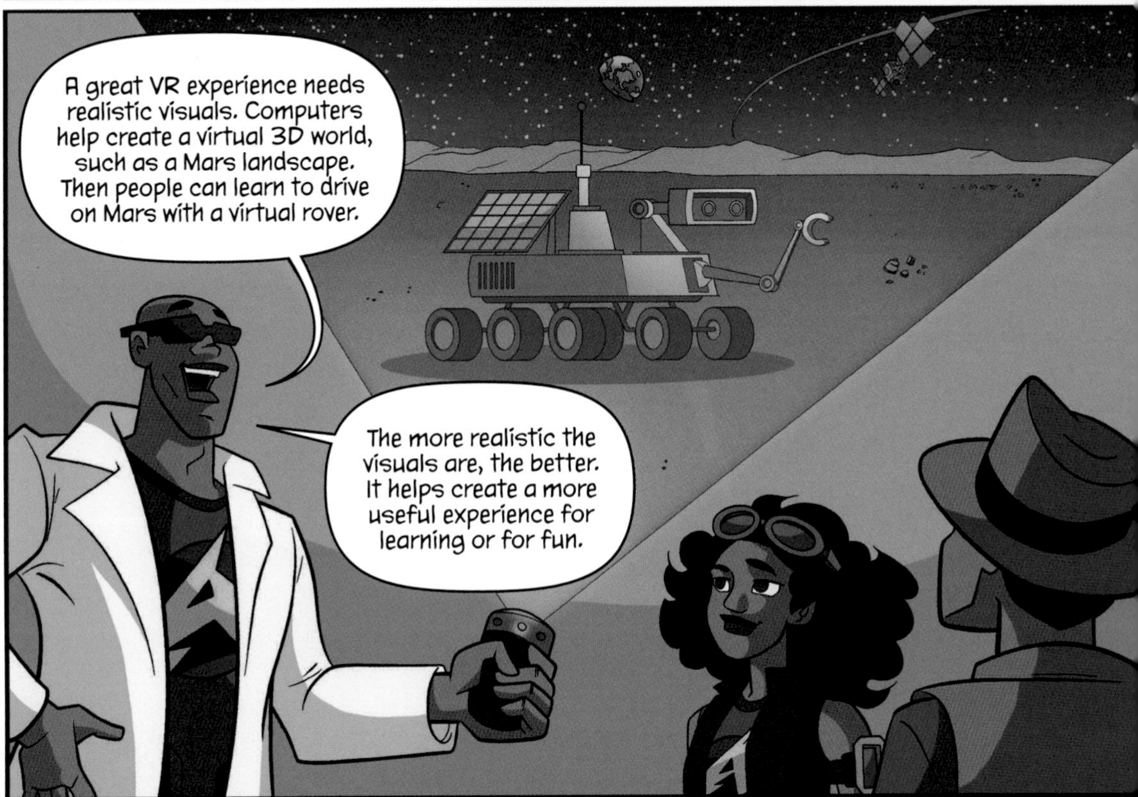
A great VR experience needs realistic visuals. Computers help create a virtual 3D world, such as a Mars landscape. Then people can learn to drive on Mars with a virtual rover.
The more realistic the visuals are, the better. It helps create a more useful experience for learning or for fun.

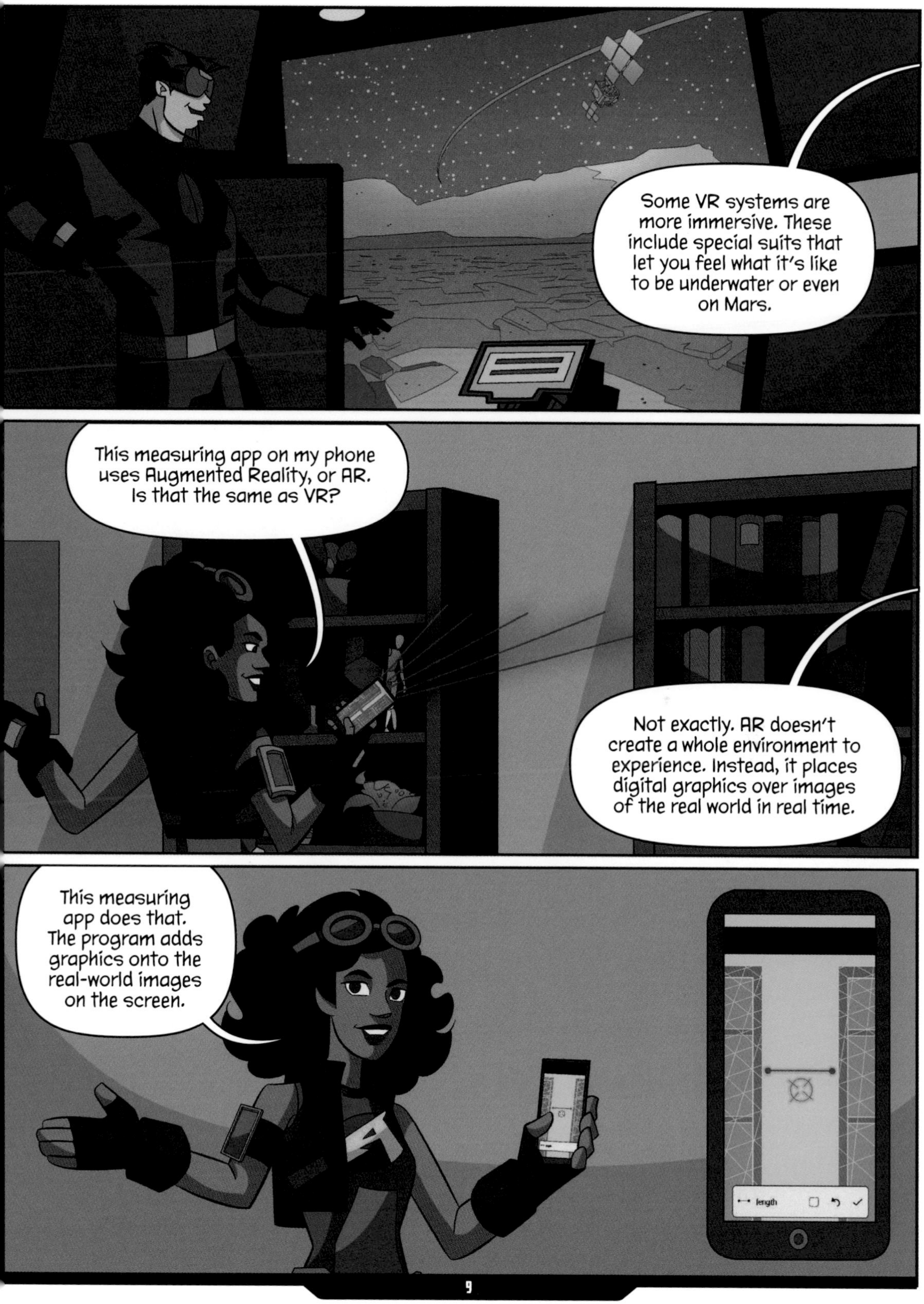
Some VR systems are more immersive. These include special suits that let you feel what it's like to be underwater or even on Mars.
This measuring app on my phone uses Augmented Reality, or AR. Is that the same as VR?
Not exactly. AR doesn't create a whole environment to experience. Instead, it places digital graphics over images of the real world in real time.
This measuring app does that. The program adds graphics onto the real-world images on the screen.
length

SECTION 2: *MAKING IT REAL*

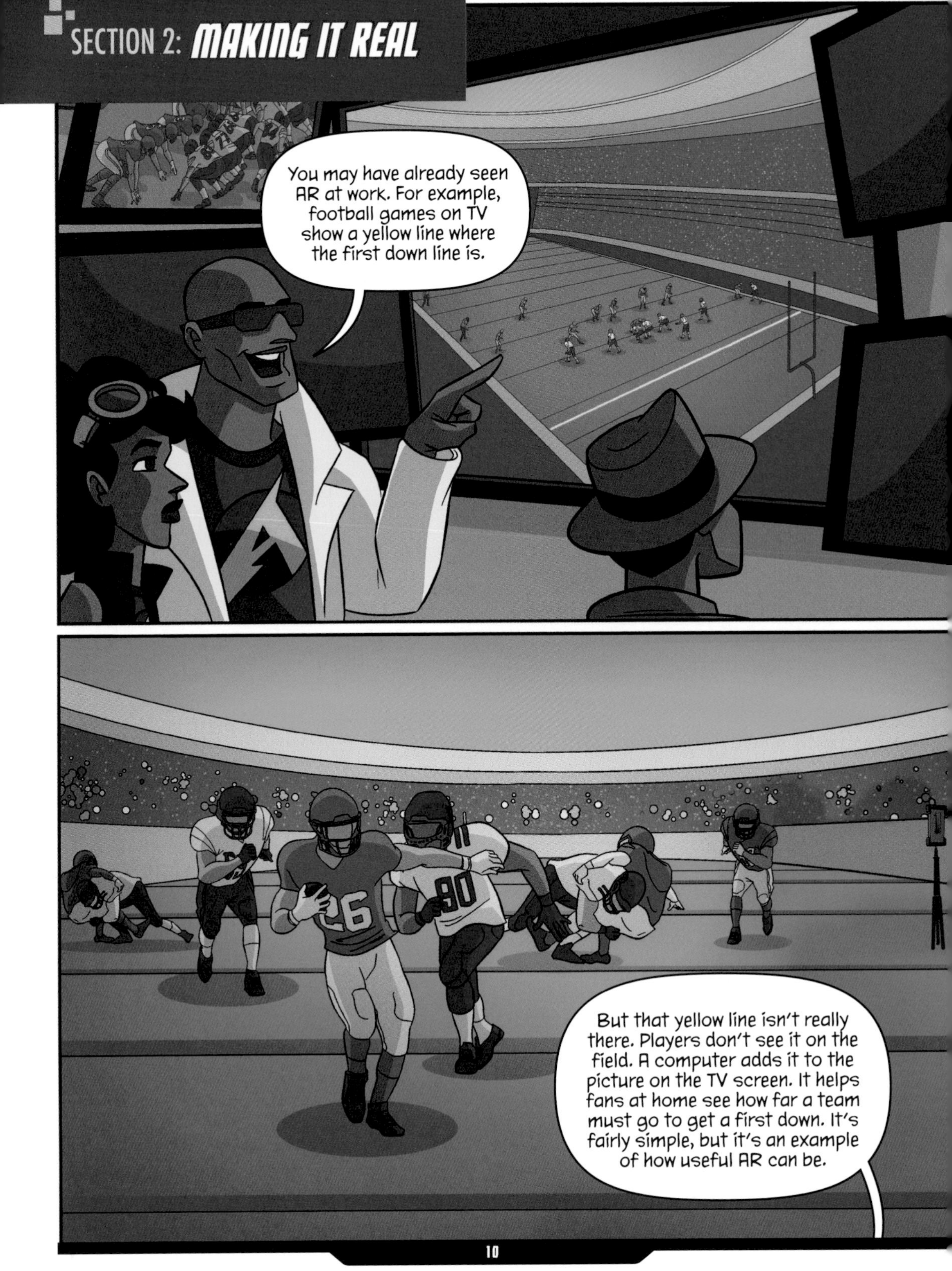
You may have already seen AR at work. For example, football games on TV show a yellow line where the first down line is.
But that yellow line isn't really there. Players don't see it on the field. A computer adds it to the picture on the TV screen. It helps fans at home see how far a team must go to get a first down. It's fairly simple, but it's an example of how useful AR can be.

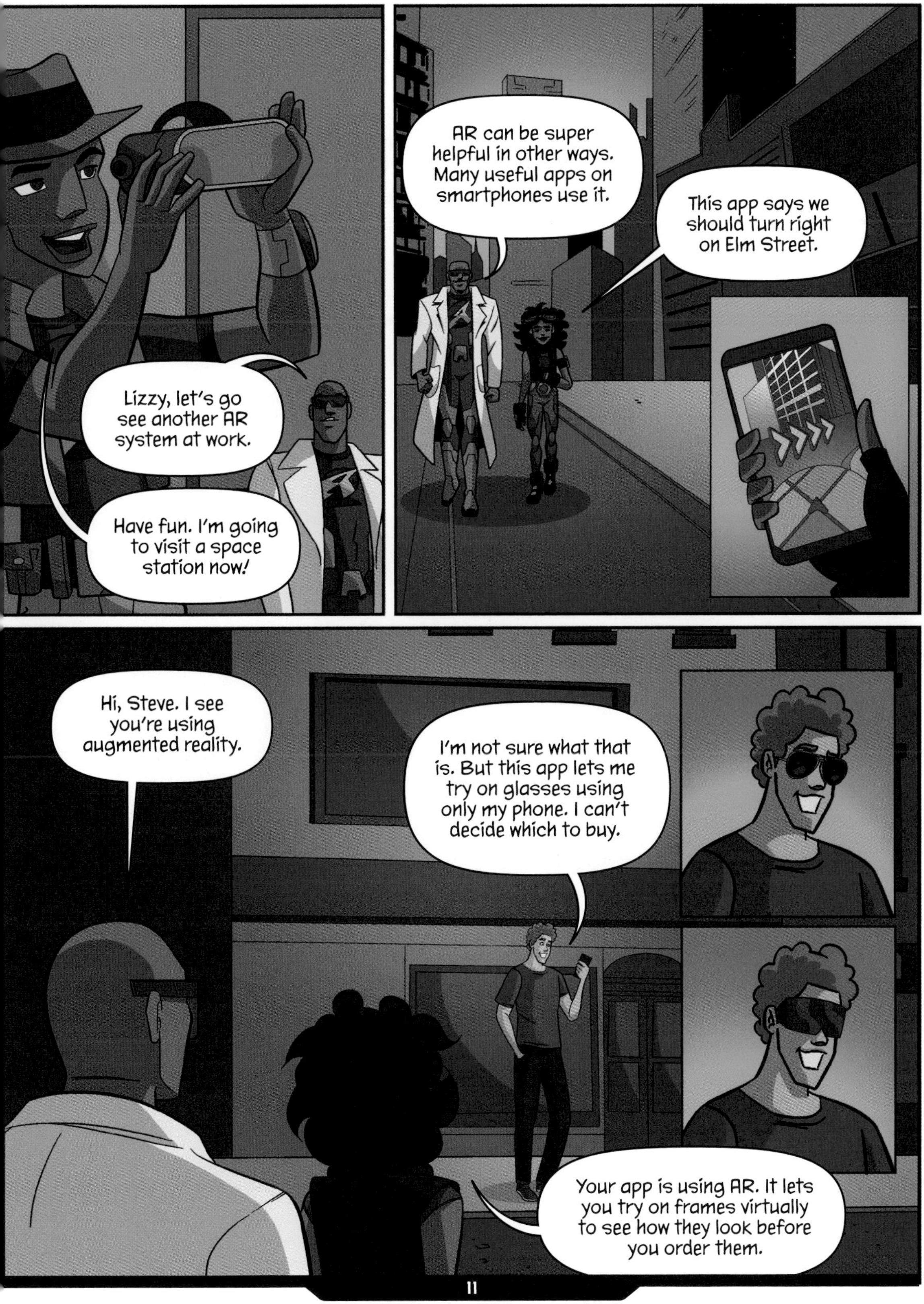

Lizzy, let's go see another AR system at work.
Have fun. I'm going to visit a space station now!
AR can be super helpful in other ways. Many useful apps on smartphones use it.
This app says we should turn right on Elm Street.
Hi, Steve. I see you're using augmented reality.
I'm not sure what that is. But this app lets me try on glasses using only my phone. I can't decide which to buy.
Your app is using AR. It lets you try on frames virtually to see how they look before you order them.

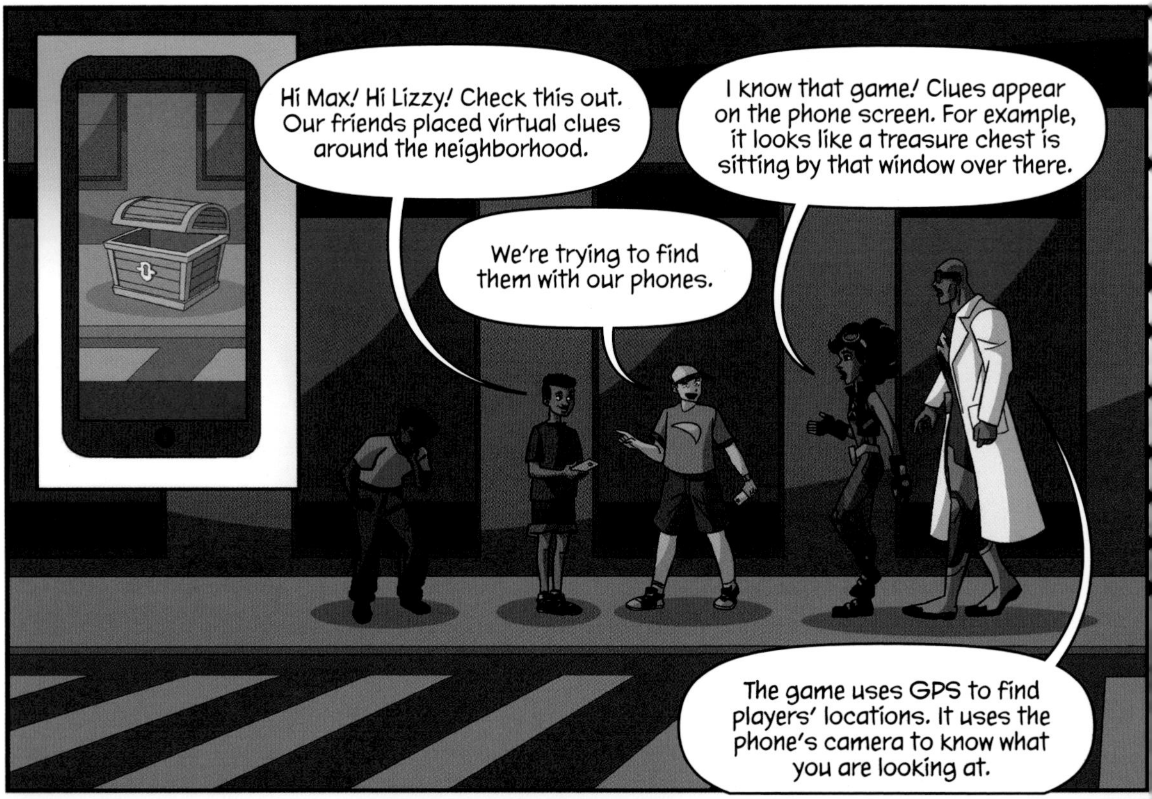
Hi Max! Hi Lizzy! Check this out. Our friends placed virtual clues around the neighborhood.
We're trying to find them with our phones.
I know that game! Clues appear on the phone screen. For example, it looks like a treasure chest is sitting by that window over there.
The game uses GPS to find players' locations. It uses the phone's camera to know what you are looking at.

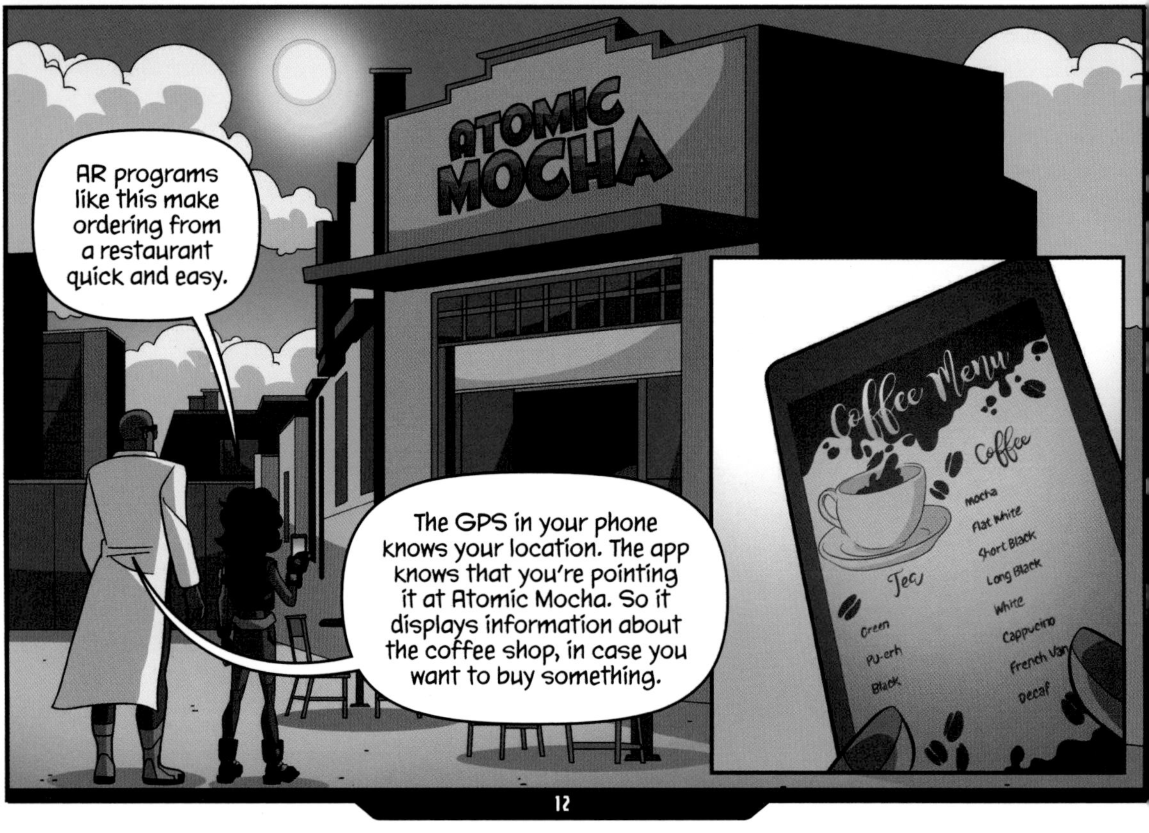
ATOMIC MOCHA
AR programs like this make ordering from a restaurant quick and easy.
The GPS in your phone knows your location. The app knows that you're pointing it at Atomic Mocha. So it displays information about the coffee shop, in case you want to buy something.
Coffee Menu
Coffee
Mocha
Flat White
Short Black
Long Black
White
Cappucino
French Van
Decaf
Tea
Green
Pu-erh
Black

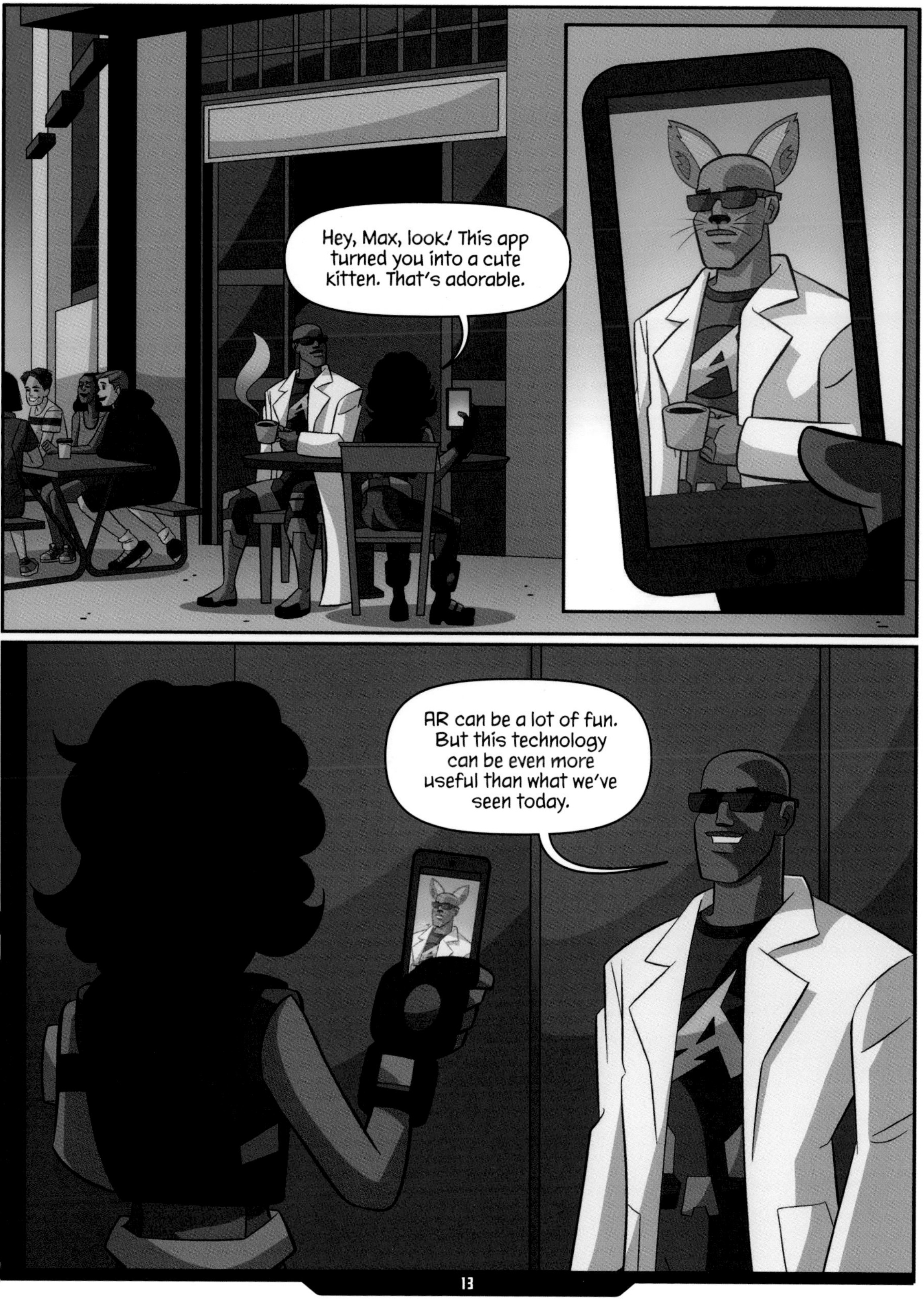
Hey, Max, look! This app turned you into a cute kitten. That's adorable.
AR can be a lot of fun. But this technology can be even more useful than what we've seen today.

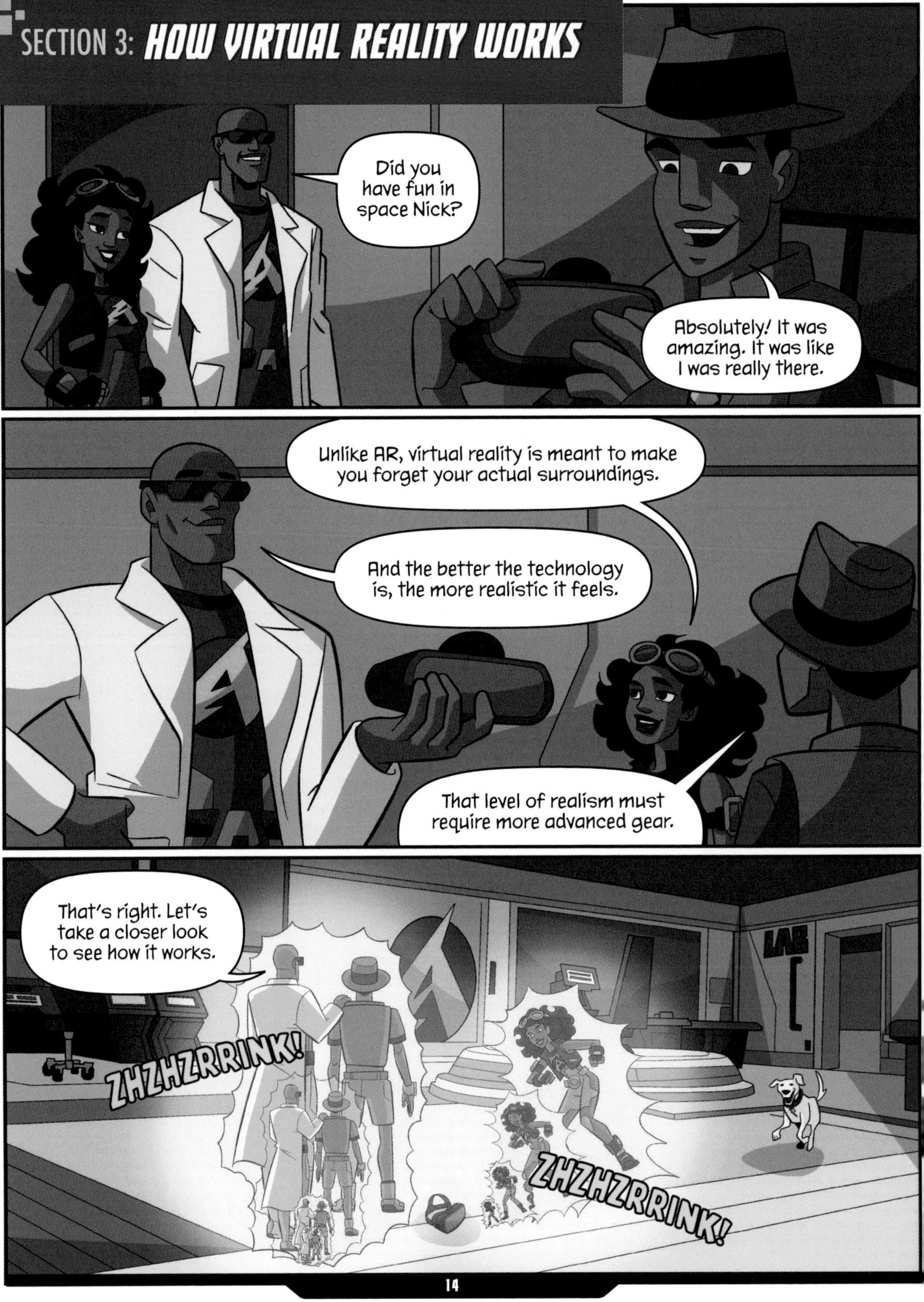
Did you have fun in space Nick?
Absolutely! It was amazing. It was like I was really there.
Unlike AR, virtual reality is meant to make you forget your actual surroundings.
And the better the technology is, the more realistic it feels.
That level of realism must require more advanced gear.
That's right. Let's take a closer look to see how it works.
ZHZHZRRINK!
LAB
ZHZHZRRINK!

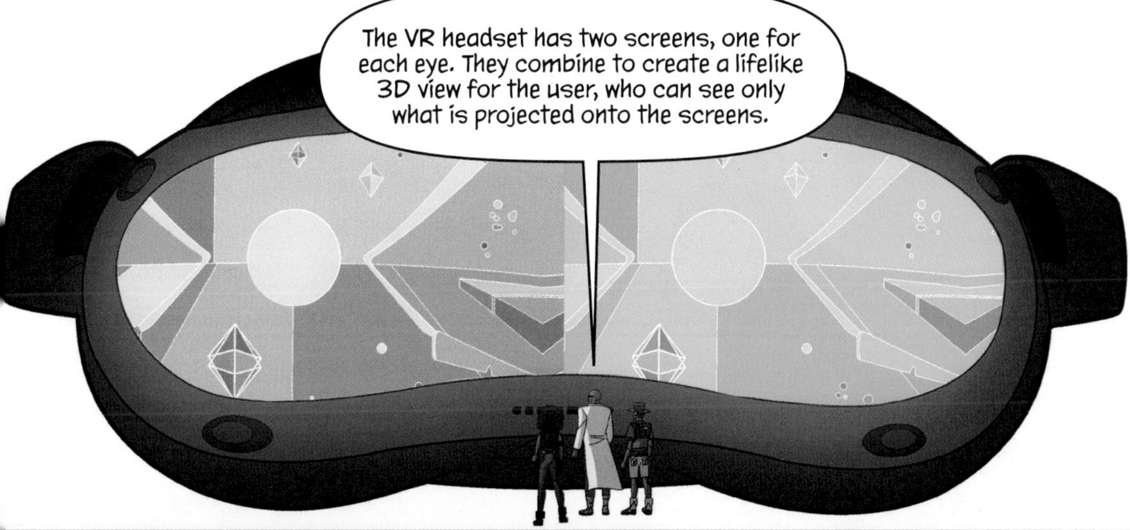
The VR headset has two screens, one for each eye. They combine to create a lifelike 3D view for the user, who can see only what is projected onto the screens.

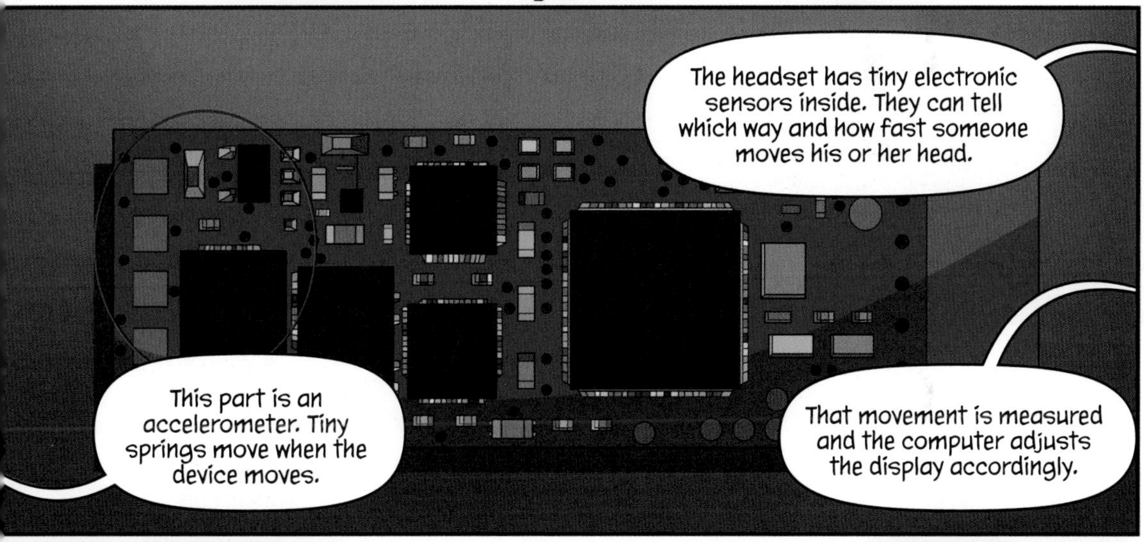
The headset has tiny electronic sensors inside. They can tell which way and how fast someone moves his or her head.
This part is an accelerometer. Tiny springs move when the device moves.
That movement is measured and the computer adjusts the display accordingly.

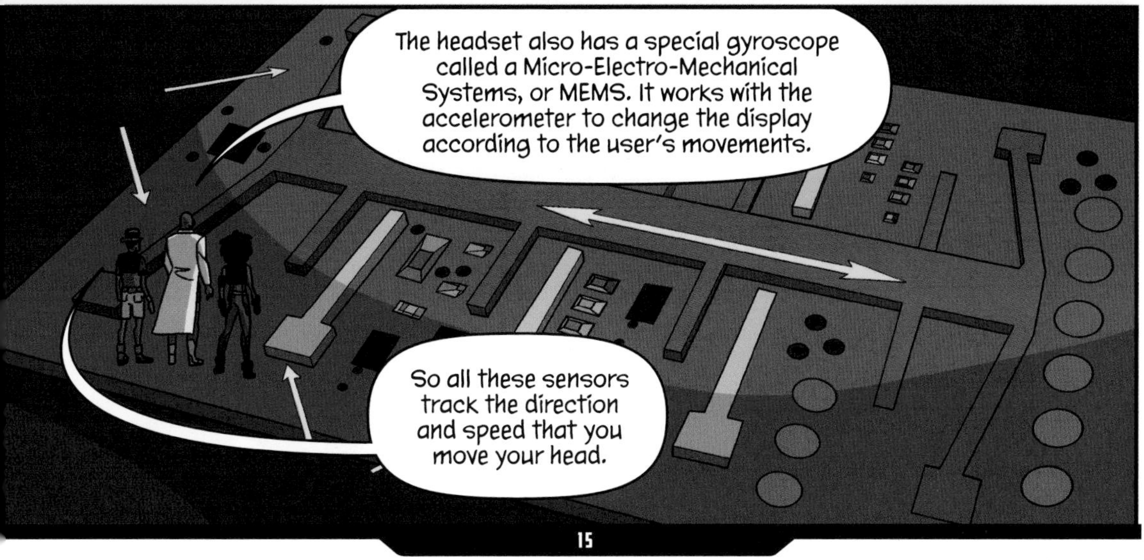
The headset also has a special gyroscope called a Micro-Electro-Mechanical Systems, or MEMS. It works with the accelerometer to change the display according to the user's movements.
So all these sensors track the direction and speed that you move your head.

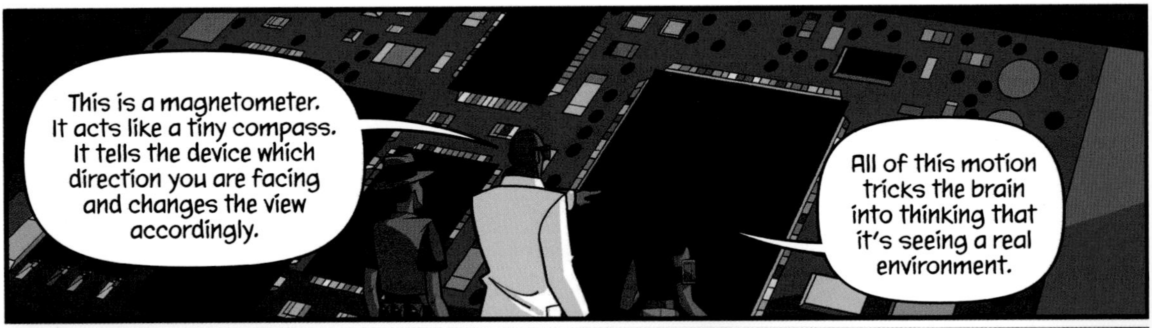
This is a magnetometer. It acts like a tiny compass. It tells the device which direction you are facing and changes the view accordingly.
All of this motion tricks the brain into thinking that it's seeing a real environment.

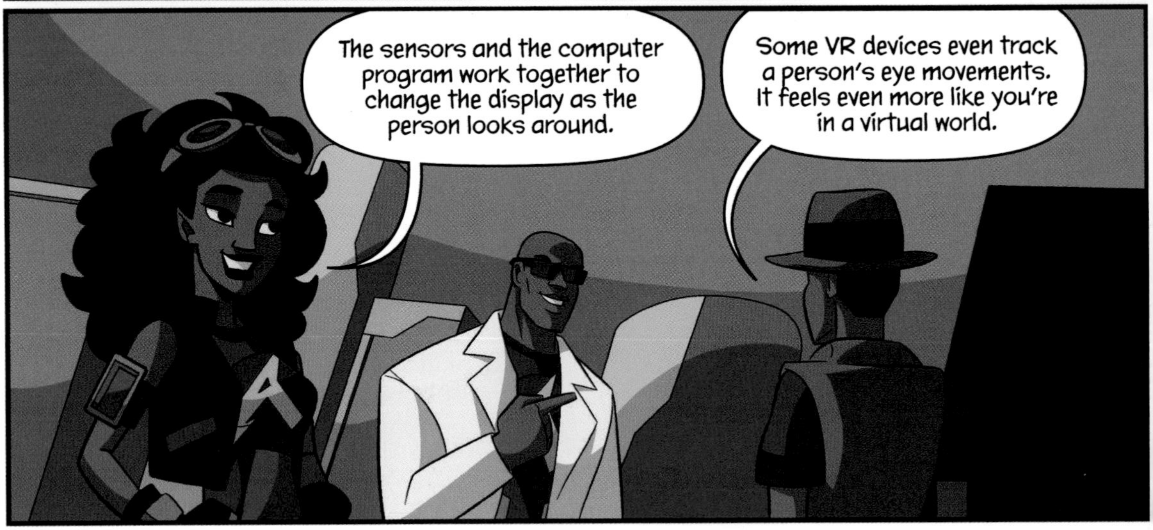
The sensors and the computer program work together to change the display as the person looks around.
Some VR devices even track a person's eye movements. It feels even more like you're in a virtual world.

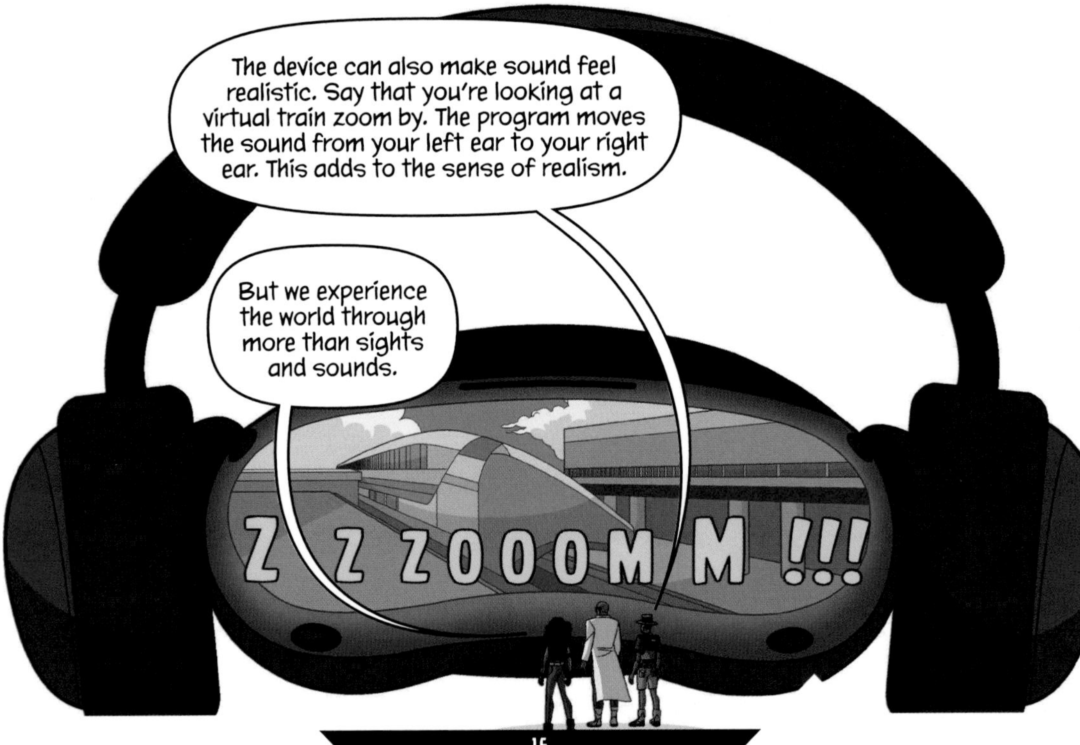
The device can also make sound feel realistic. Say that you're looking at a virtual train zoom by. The program moves the sound from your left ear to your right ear. This adds to the sense of realism.
But we experience the world through more than sights and sounds.
Z Z ZOOOM M M !!!

In the Space Station program, I could grab objects. How does that work in a virtual world?

The controllers have sensors all over them.

Cameras in the headset detect them and track the movement of the controllers.

The program then shows that movement as your hands on the screen. The controllers' buttons and triggers let you grab things and move them around.

But basic controllers aren't sensitive enough for a truly immersive experience.

Simulating the full motion of a human hand is very complex.

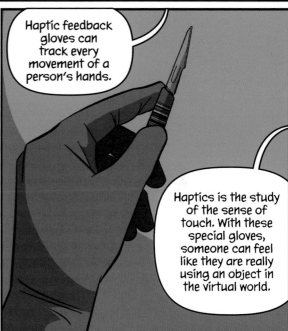

Haptic feedback gloves can track every movement of a person's hands.

Haptics is the study of the sense of touch. With these special gloves, someone can feel like they are really using an object in the virtual world.

SMART TAPPING

Many devices, such as smartphones, already use haptic feedback. It's the tiny vibration you feel when you tap a button or the keyboard on a phone screen. It lets you instantly know that you've clicked on something.

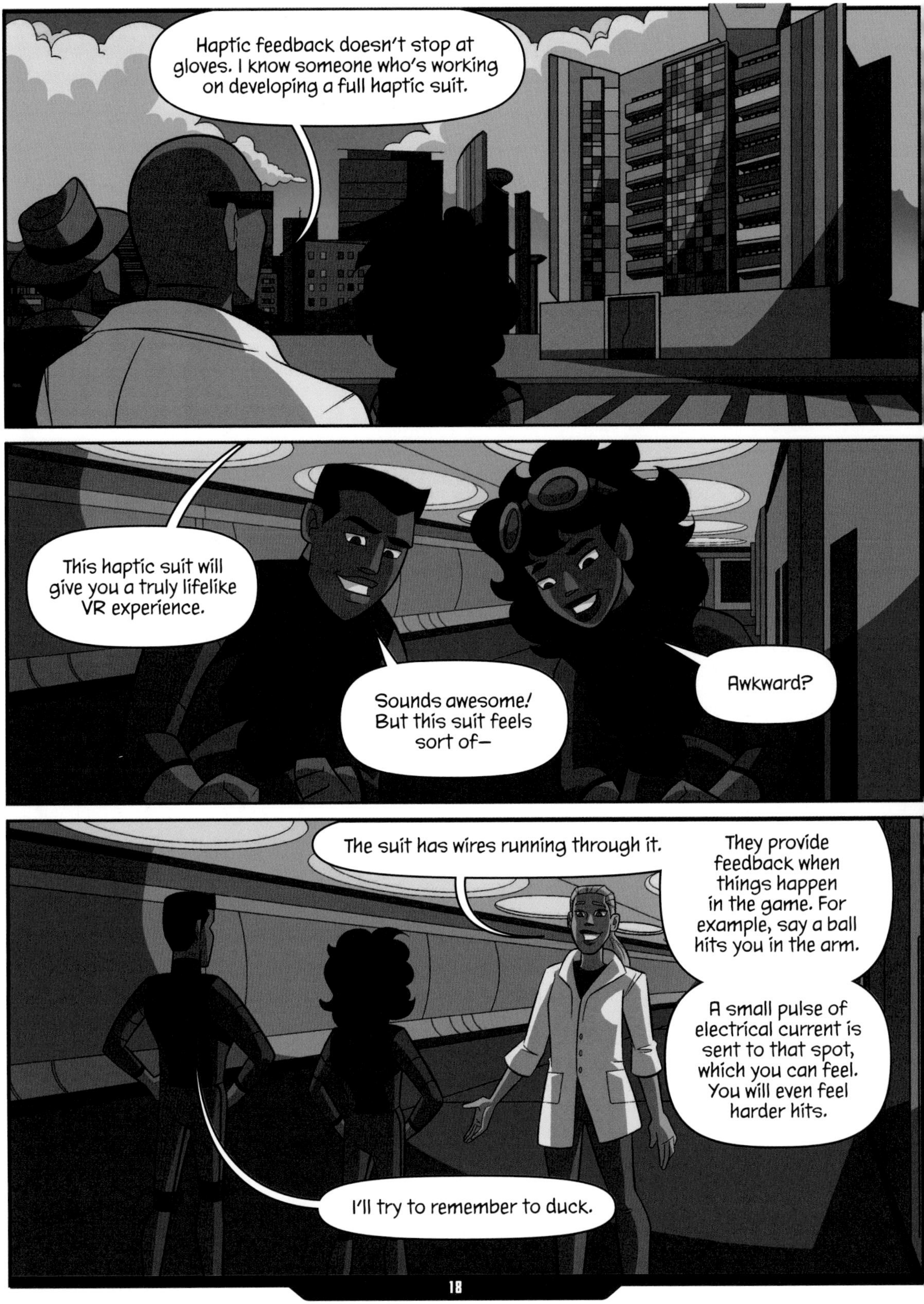

Haptic feedback doesn't stop at gloves. I know someone who's working on developing a full haptic suit.
This haptic suit will give you a truly lifelike VR experience.
Sounds awesome! But this suit feels sort of—
Awkward?
The suit has wires running through it.
They provide feedback when things happen in the game. For example, say a ball hits you in the arm.
A small pulse of electrical current is sent to that spot, which you can feel. You will even feel harder hits.
I'll try to remember to duck.

WHAP!

Ouch! It feels a bit like wearing a scuba diving suit. But I felt that ball hit me in the shoulder!

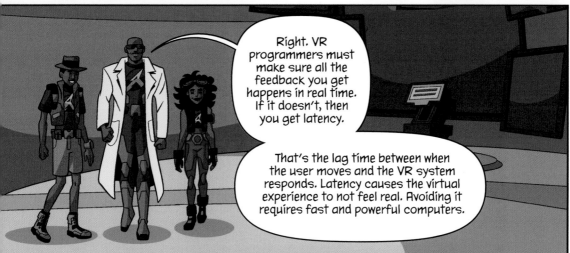

You're not sore after being hit by a virtual ball, are you?

Not at all! It just felt like a little vibration. But it was right where I saw the ball hit me.

What if you didn't feel the ball hit you right away?

It wouldn't seem realistic.

Right. VR programmers must make sure all the feedback you get happens in real time. If it doesn't, then you get latency.

That's the lag time between when the user moves and the VR system responds. Latency causes the virtual experience to not feel real. Avoiding it requires fast and powerful computers.

SECTION 4: THE FUTURE OF VR

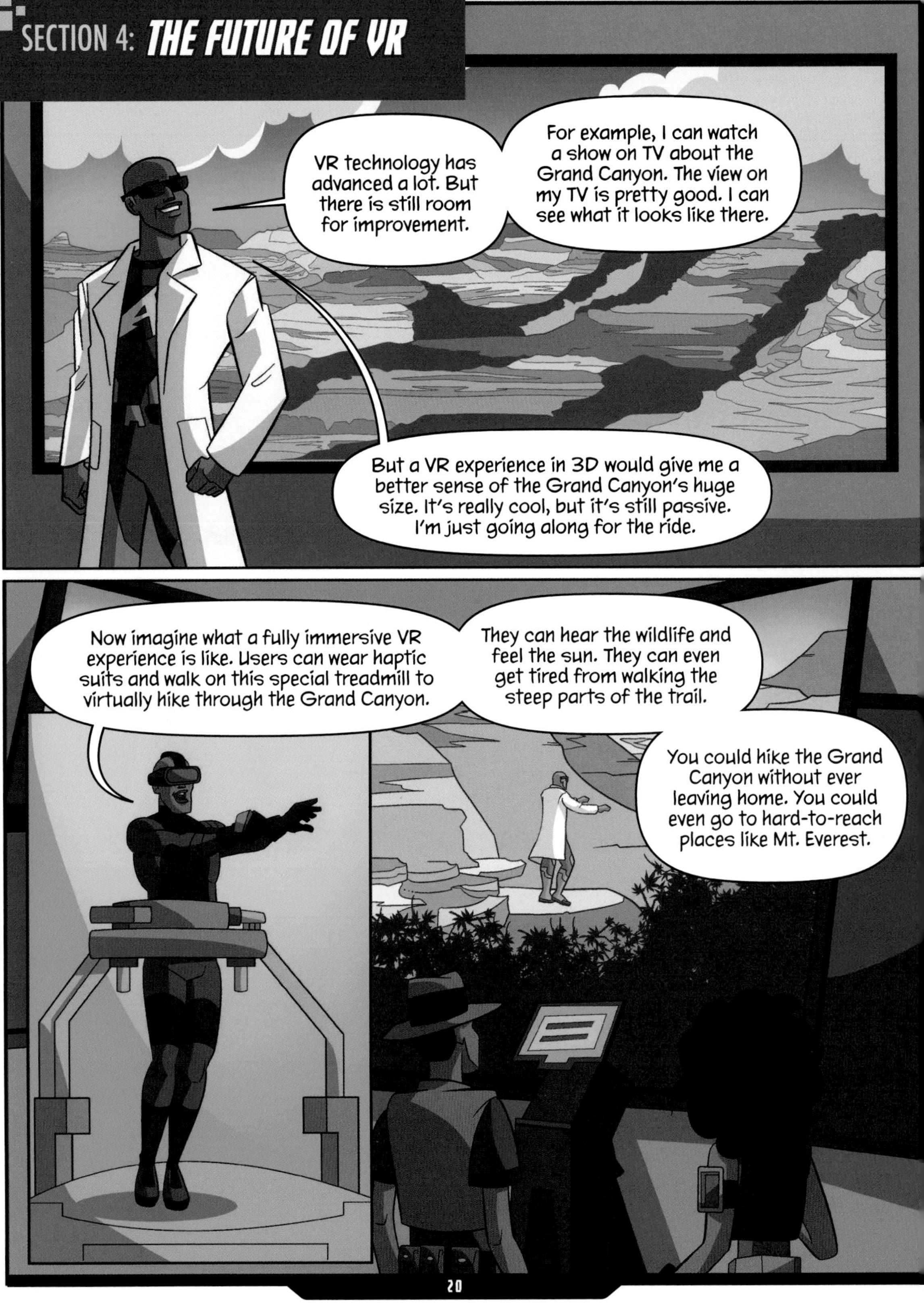
VR technology has advanced a lot. But there is still room for improvement.
For example, I can watch a show on TV about the Grand Canyon. The view on my TV is pretty good. I can see what it looks like there.
But a VR experience in 3D would give me a better sense of the Grand Canyon's huge size. It's really cool, but it's still passive. I'm just going along for the ride.
Now imagine what a fully immersive VR experience is like. Users can wear haptic suits and walk on this special treadmill to virtually hike through the Grand Canyon.
They can hear the wildlife and feel the sun. They can even get tired from walking the steep parts of the trail.
You could hike the Grand Canyon without ever leaving home. You could even go to hard-to-reach places like Mt. Everest.

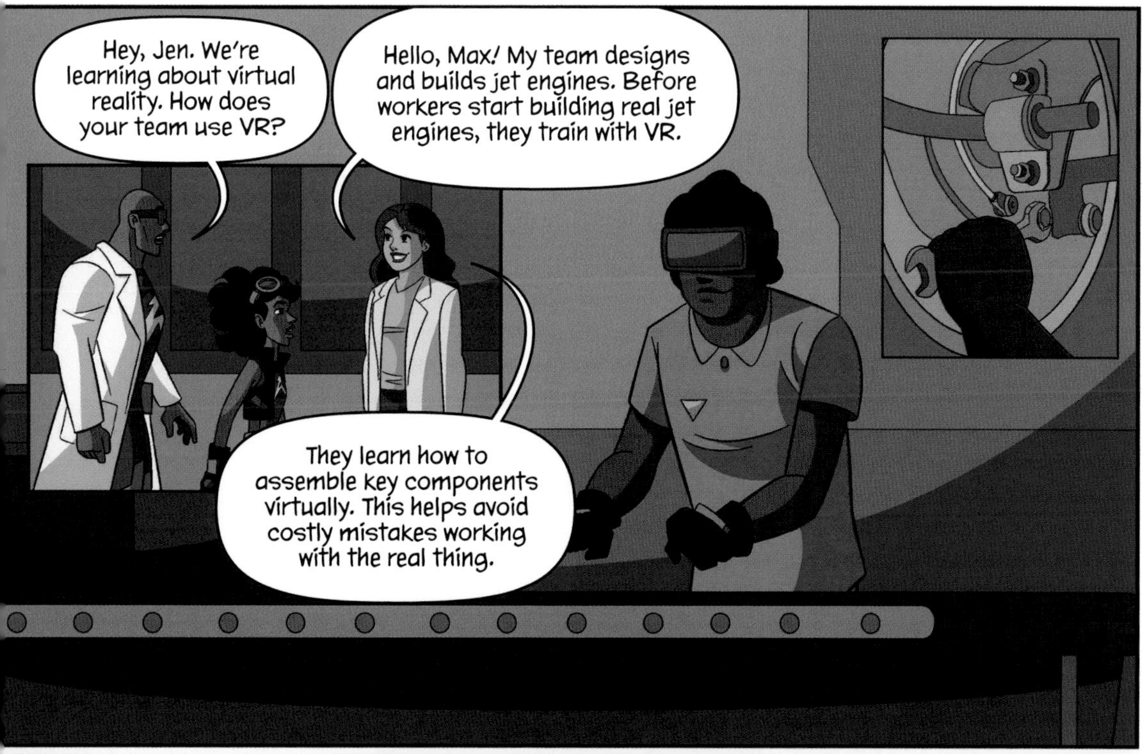
Hey, Jen. We're learning about virtual reality. How does your team use VR?
Hello, Max! My team designs and builds jet engines. Before workers start building real jet engines, they train with VR.
They learn how to assemble key components virtually. This helps avoid costly mistakes working with the real thing.

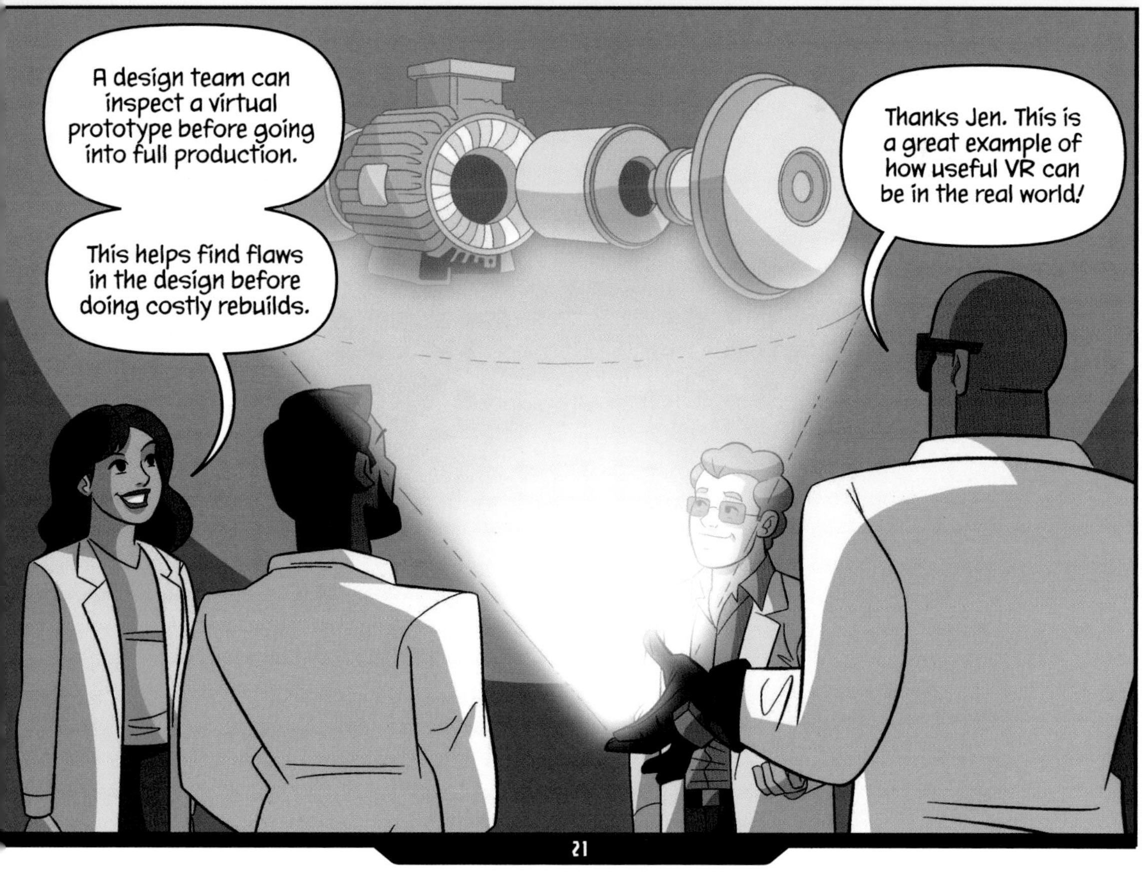
A design team can inspect a virtual prototype before going into full production.
This helps find flaws in the design before doing costly rebuilds.
Thanks Jen. This is a great example of how useful VR can be in the real world!

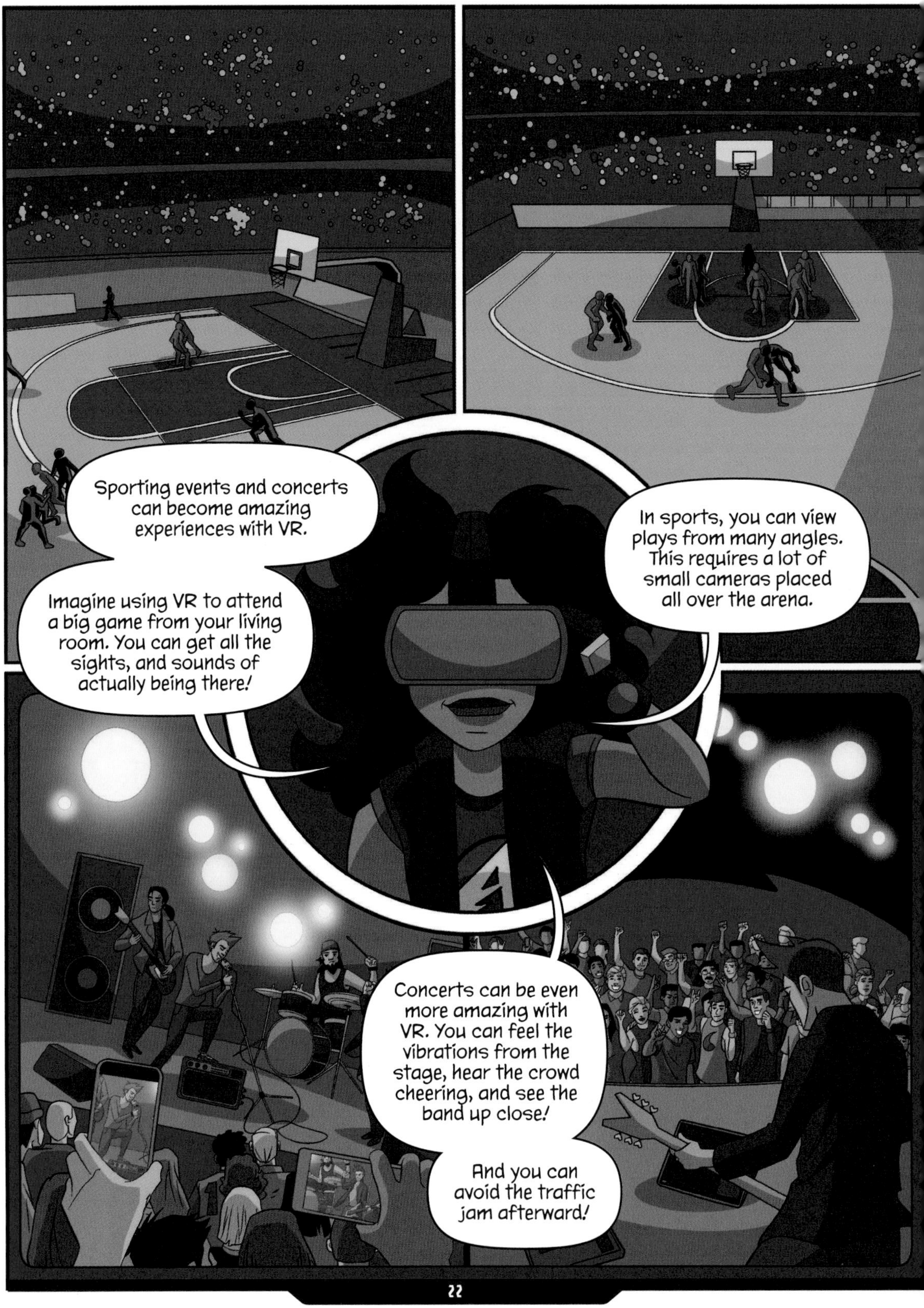

Sporting events and concerts can become amazing experiences with VR.
Imagine using VR to attend a big game from your living room. You can get all the sights, and sounds of actually being there!
In sports, you can view plays from many angles. This requires a lot of small cameras placed all over the arena.
Concerts can be even more amazing with VR. You can feel the vibrations from the stage, hear the crowd cheering, and see the band up close!
And you can avoid the traffic jam afterward!

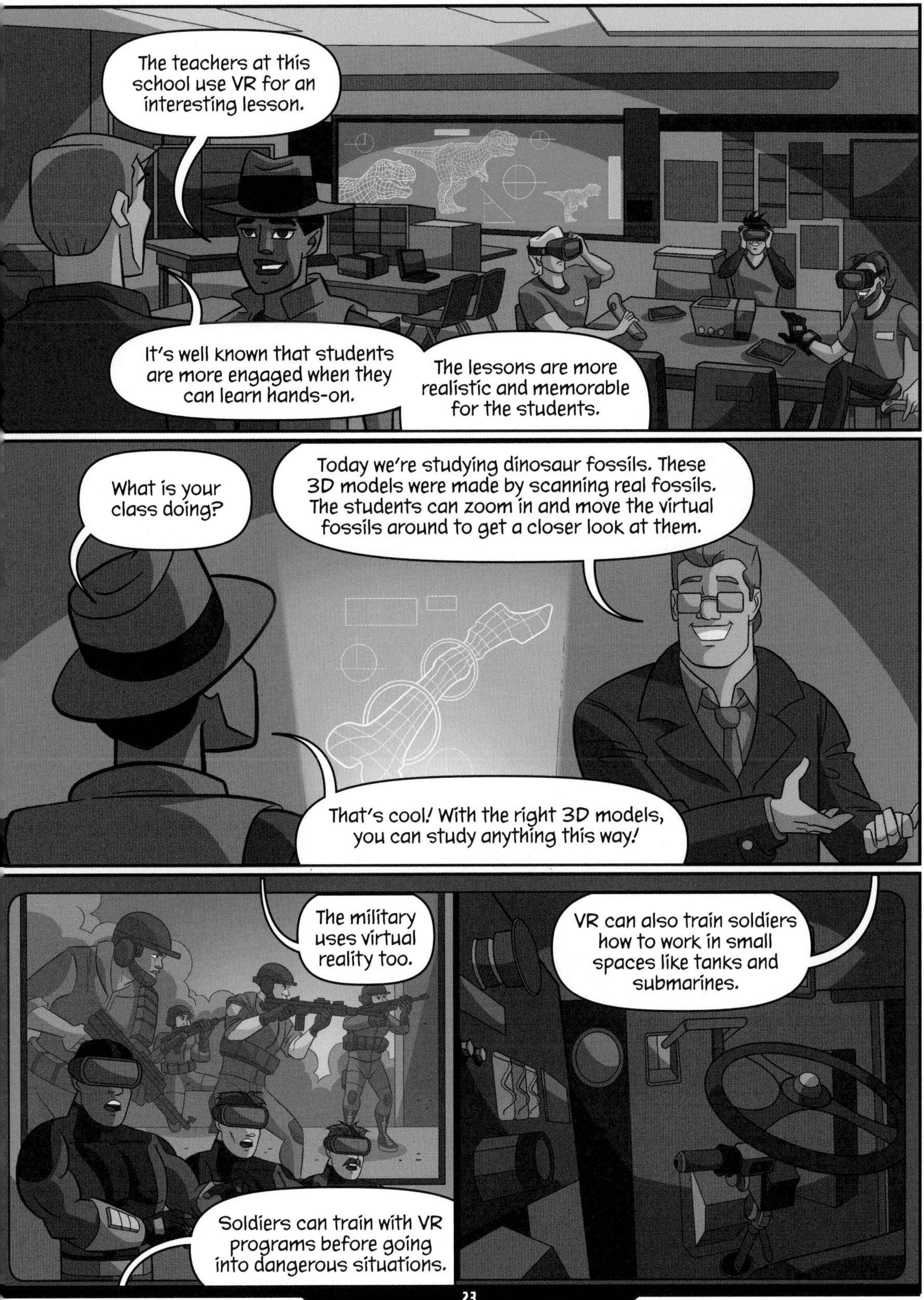
The teachers at this school use VR for an interesting lesson.
It's well known that students are more engaged when they can learn hands-on.
The lessons are more realistic and memorable for the students.
What is your class doing?
Today we're studying dinosaur fossils. These 3D models were made by scanning real fossils. The students can zoom in and move the virtual fossils around to get a closer look at them.
That's cool! With the right 3D models, you can study anything this way!
The military uses virtual reality too.
Soldiers can train with VR programs before going into dangerous situations.
VR can also train soldiers how to work in small spaces like tanks and submarines.

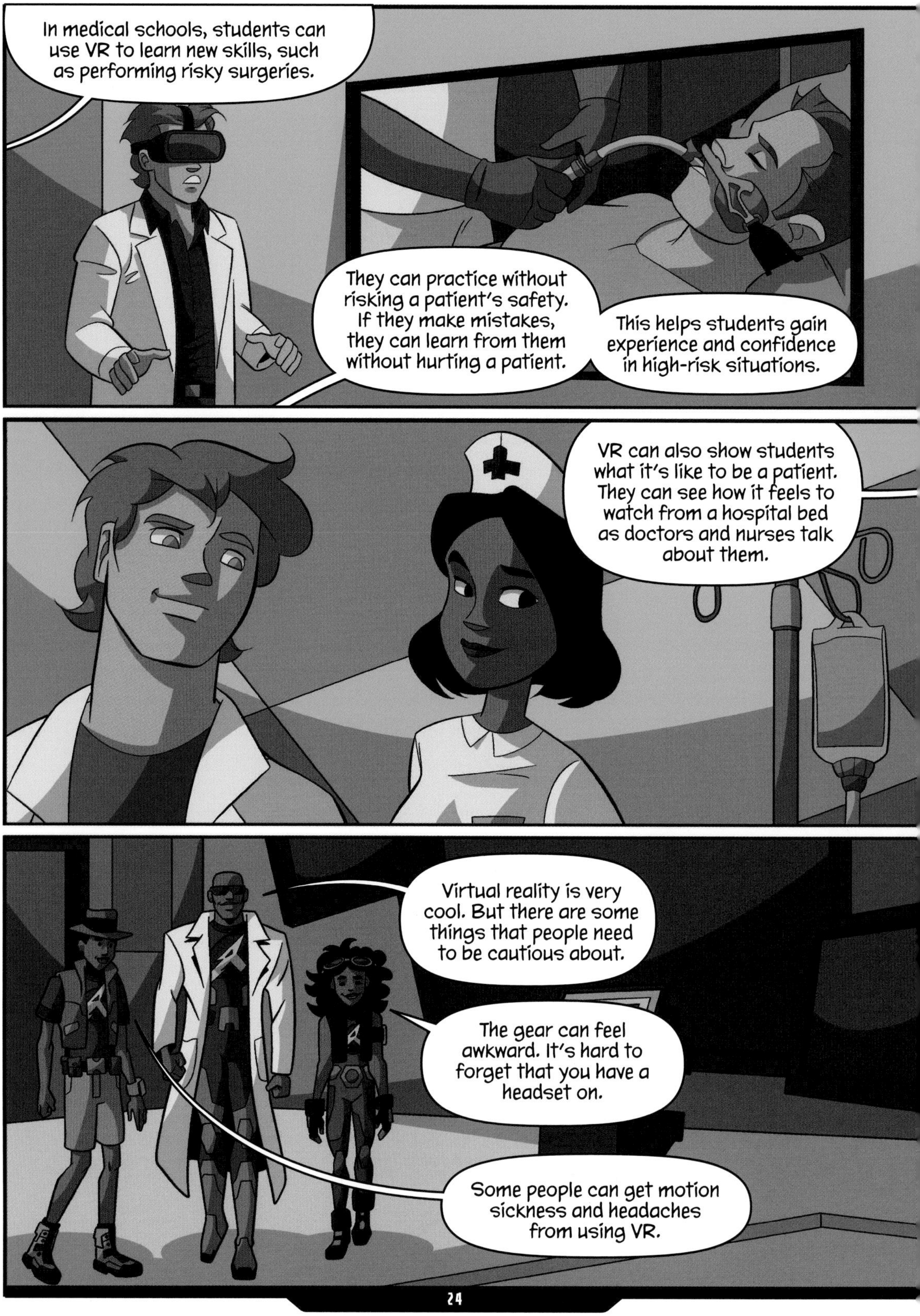
In medical schools, students can use VR to learn new skills, such as performing risky surgeries.
They can practice without risking a patient's safety. If they make mistakes, they can learn from them without hurting a patient.
This helps students gain experience and confidence in high-risk situations.
VR can also show students what it's like to be a patient. They can see how it feels to watch from a hospital bed as doctors and nurses talk about them.
Virtual reality is very cool. But there are some things that people need to be cautious about.
The gear can feel awkward. It's hard to forget that you have a headset on.
Some people can get motion sickness and headaches from using VR.

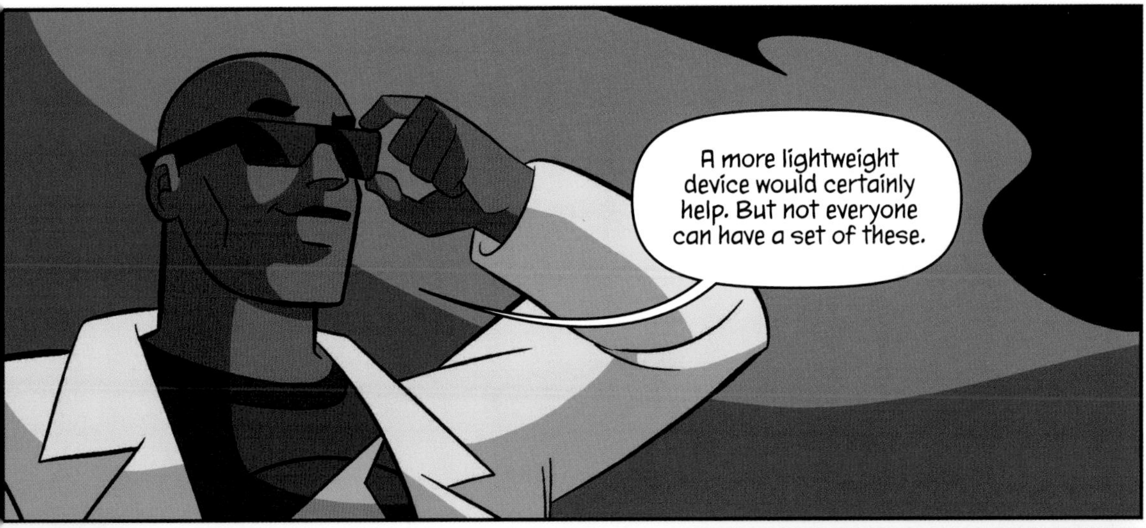
A more lightweight device would certainly help. But not everyone can have a set of these.

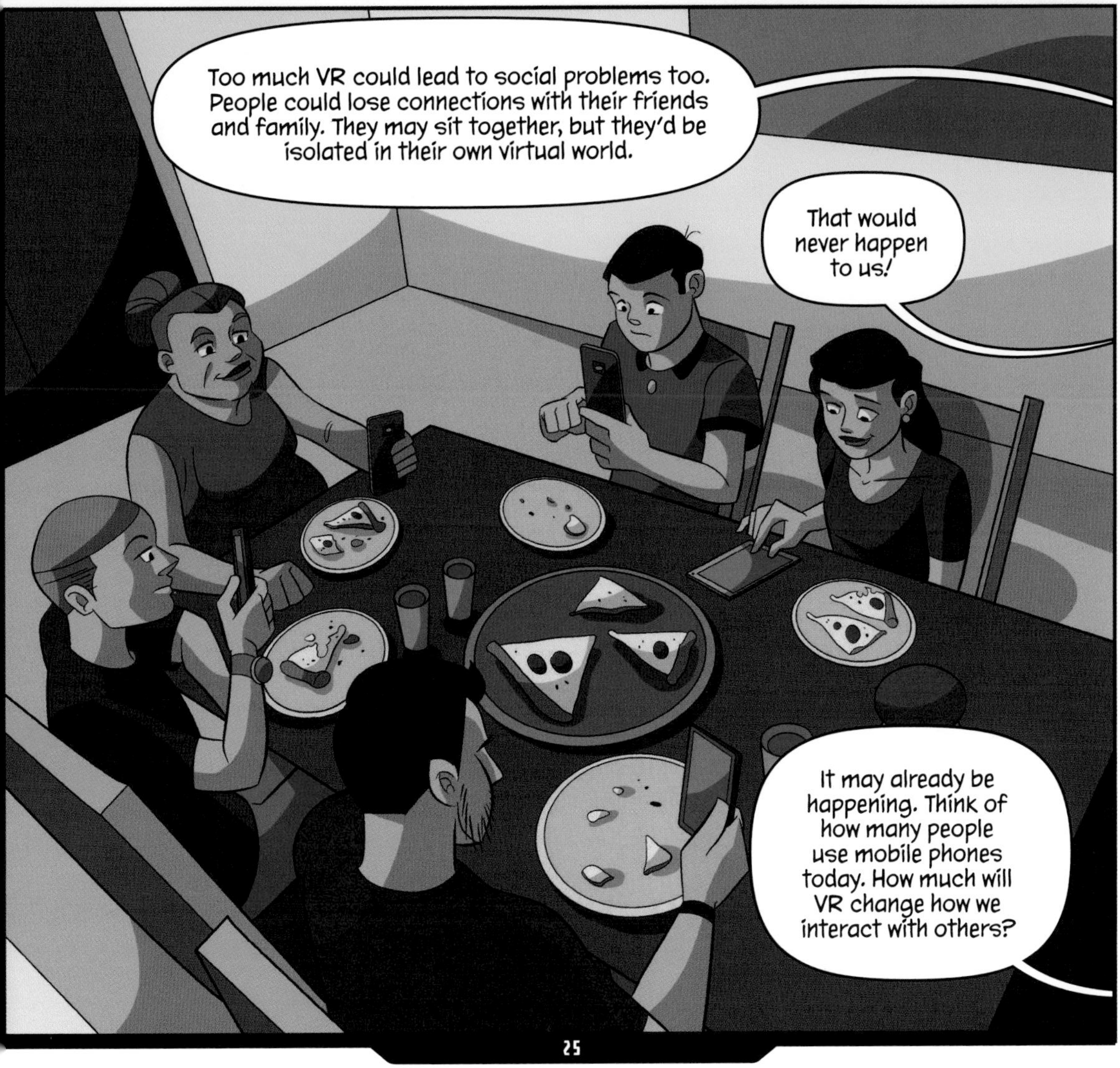
Too much VR could lead to social problems too. People could lose connections with their friends and family. They may sit together, but they'd be isolated in their own virtual world.
That would never happen to us!
It may already be happening. Think of how many people use mobile phones today. How much will VR change how we interact with others?

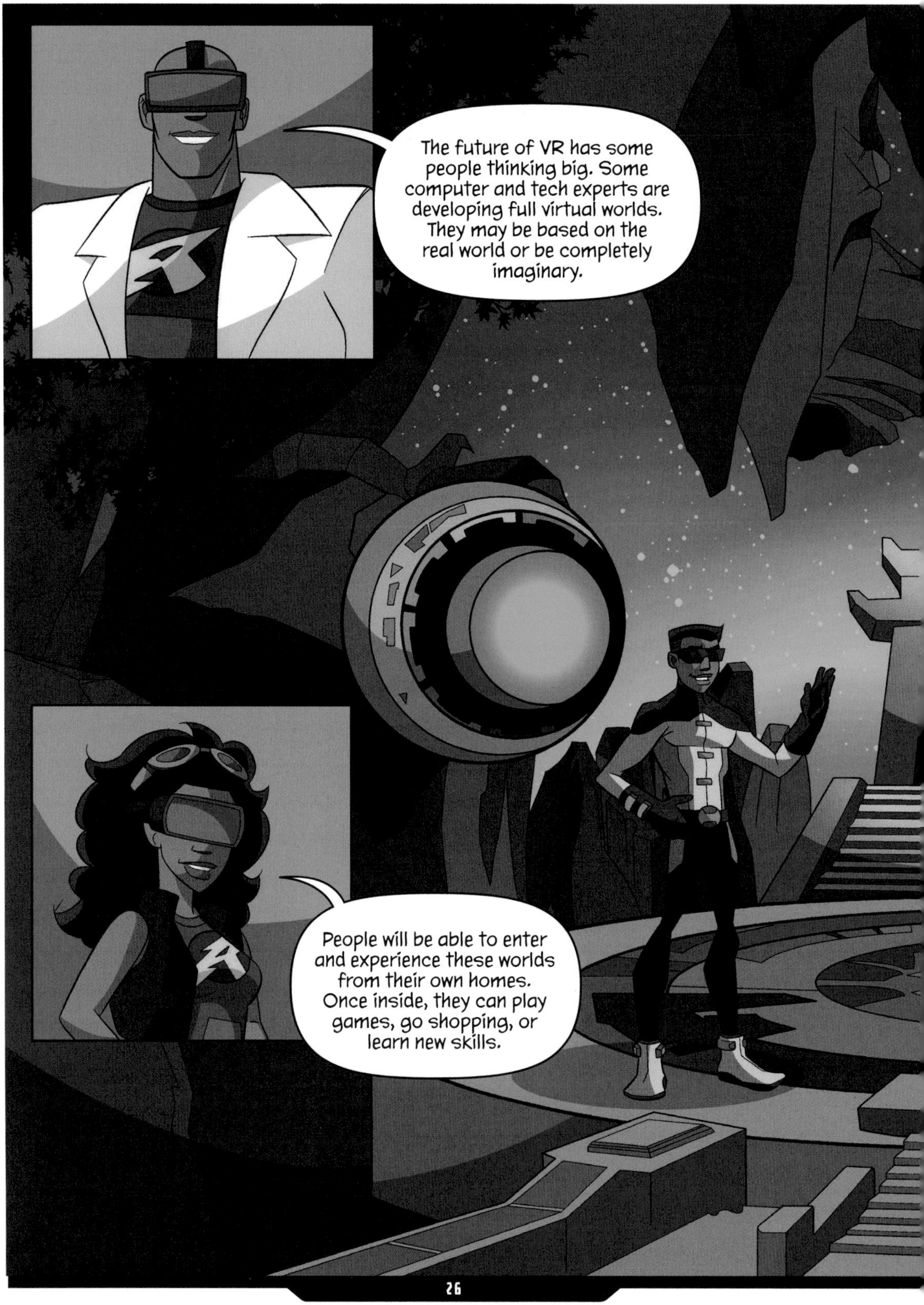
The future of VR has some people thinking big. Some computer and tech experts are developing full virtual worlds. They may be based on the real world or be completely imaginary.
People will be able to enter and experience these worlds from their own homes. Once inside, they can play games, go shopping, or learn new skills.

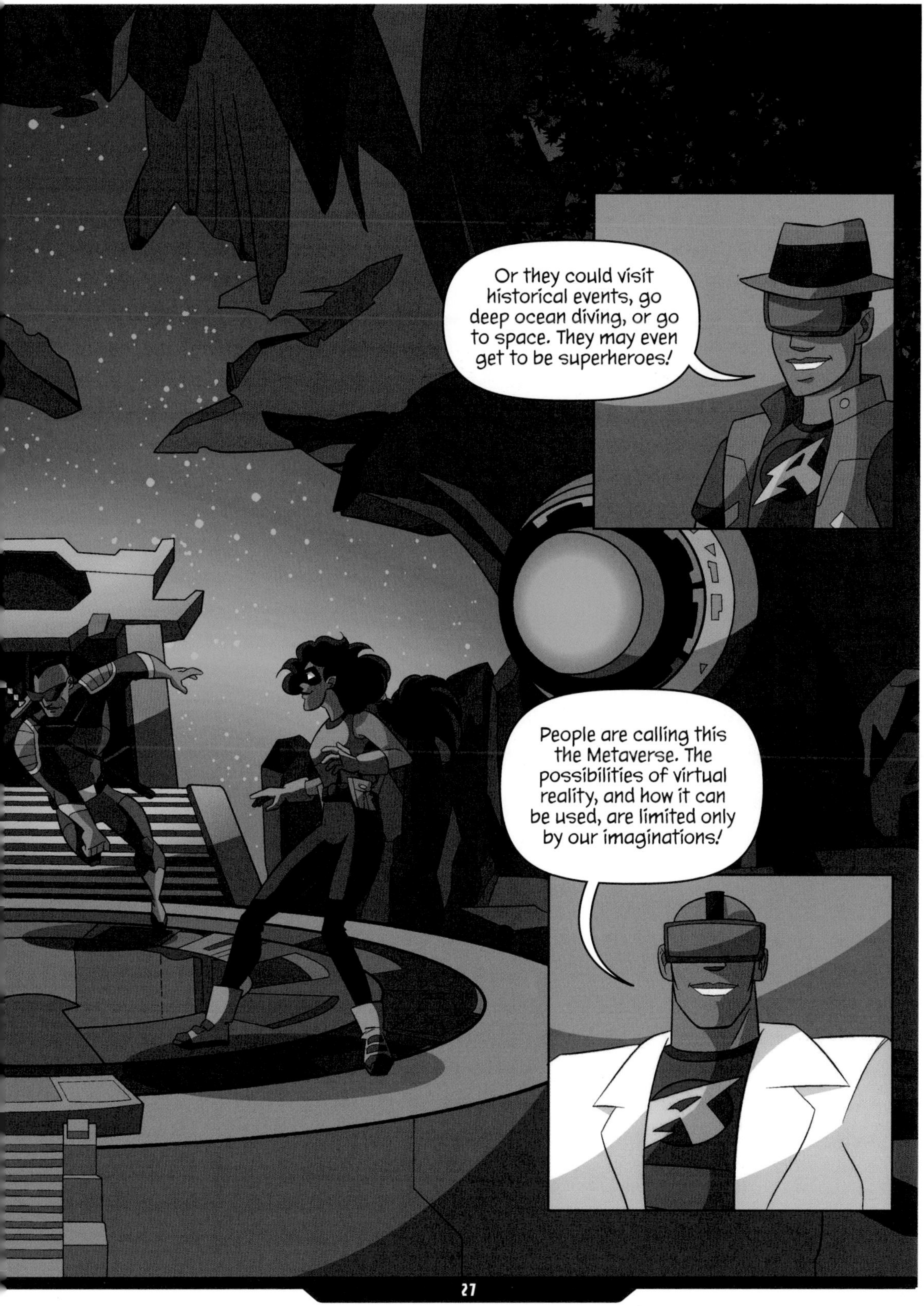
Or they could visit historical events, go deep ocean diving, or go to space. They may even get to be superheroes!
People are calling this the Metaverse. The possibilities of virtual reality, and how it can be used, are limited only by our imaginations!

MORE ABOUT VIRTUAL AND AUGMENTED REALITY

Researchers are developing new VR gear that's more user friendly, such as lightweight glasses instead of the bulky headsets. There's even something called a virtual retina display. It will be able to project an image right to a person's eyes!

Sports simulators use VR tech. Golf simulators use cameras and sensors to track the player's swing and path of the ball. 3D models of golf courses allow players to play a real course indoors. No walking or golf carts needed! Other sports simulators can be used by pro players to analyze their play and get ready for the next game.

VR may make shopping easier. You could virtually walk through a store, put items in a virtual cart, pay, and then have the items delivered to your home. Shoppers could visualize how new furniture will look in their house before lugging it home. Some programs even let you try different paint colors for your house before you decide what to use.

If a VR user notices too much latency, they experience something called swimming. It's more than just distracting. It's one of the causes of motion sickness in VR.

VR could cause privacy problems. If people use VR glasses in public, they could easily record video without others knowing it. It could also be easier for a person's private information to be stolen.

Augmented Reality apps for smartphones can do many things. They can help you get directions, draw lines in virtual space, study history, go stargazing, learn new languages, and play games on a tabletop or the floor of your living room.

There are many immersive VR games currently available. You can ride extreme roller coasters, play team games, play fighting games, try adventure games with storylines, or just play simple table tennis.

There are also many other VR adventures people can try. You can test your fear of heights, or explore documentaries about dinosaurs or the deep ocean. You can also see what it's like to fly like a bird or even try sky diving without jumping out of a plane!

GLOSSARY

accelerometer (ak-sel-uh-ROM-ih-tuhr)—an instrument used to measure the increase and decrease in speed of an object

Augmented Reality (AWG-men-tuhd ree-AL-ih-tee)—a computer-made image or data laid over an image of a real-world environment

GPS (GEE PEE ESS)—an electronic tool that uses satellite signals to find the location of an object; GPS is also called Global Positioning System

gyroscope (JAHY-ruh-skohp)—a device that contains a spinning wheel used to measure the direction of motion

haptic feedback (HAP-tik FEED-bak)—computer-generated impulses or vibrations that simulate physical sensations while interacting with an electronic device

immersive (ih-MUR-siv)—relating to technology that creates a realistic experience

latency (LAYT-ehn-see)—the time delay between a real-world action and the response of a computer program in a simulation

magnetometer (mag-nih-TOM-ih-tuhr)—an instrument for measuring the intensity of a magnetic field

simulator (SIM-yuh-lay-tuhr)—a device designed to reproduce a real-world environment or situation

virtual (VUR-choo-uhl)—relating to objects or environments created within a computer program

READ MORE

Challoner, Jack. *Virtual Reality*. New York: DK Publishing, 2017.

Kuromiya, Jun. *Future of Entertainment*. Minneapolis: Lerner Publications, 2021.

Rathburn, Betsy. *Virtual Reality Gaming*. Minneapolis, MN: Bellwether Media Inc., 2021.

INTERNET SITES

Time for Kids: What is the Metaverse?
timeforkids.com/g56/what-is-the-metaverse/?rl=en-860

Virtual Reality Facts for Kids
kids.kiddle.co/Virtual_reality

Virtual Reality for Kids
moonpreneur.com/blog/virtual-reality-for-kids/

ABOUT THE AUTHOR

Thomas K. Adamson has written many nonfiction books for kids. Sports, math, science, cool vehicles, a little of everything! When not writing, he likes to hike, watch movies, eat pizza, and of course, read. He lives in South Dakota with his wife, two sons, and a Morkie named Moe.

ABOUT THE ILLUSTRATOR

Daniel Pedrosa was born in Araraquara, a quiet town in São Paulo, Brazil. Since he was a child he has always had an interest in art. At the age of ten, his older brother gave him his first superhero comic. It was then he decided that drawing comics would be his profession. In 2010, he began his professional career doing comic strips for newspapers and drawing children's supplements for tabloids and magazines. Today Daniel creates colorful art for Criptozoik, Tildawave, Capstone, 137 Studios, and produces advertising material for the largest Honda Motors store in Brazil.